Critical Thinking: Beginners guide to advanced critical thinking concepts for problem-solving, decision making and goal achievement

Chapter 1: The Six Stages of Critical Thinkers

Think back to when you were in school. Do you remember learning how to think critically? You were probably taught these skills in your English class while learning how to read and comprehend information. And while now you may do it automatically, at the time it was a process. A sometimes slow, painful process. Why is that? Because unfortunately, many educators do not know how to properly teach critical thinking skills (because they weren't taught either).

The improved intellectual quality of work happens when critical thinking is taught and nurtured in developmental stages. That is to say that the concept of critical thinking is not one linear path, but preferably several steps to achieve a deep understanding and comprehension of a particular concept.

If any of these stages are skipped or overlooked, it can lead to a disconnect between thought and analysis. When this disconnect happens, gaps are created in the brain which makes it difficult to move into a deeper thinking pattern.

This book intends to approach the concept of critical thinking from an intellectual standpoint, not a psychological one. So when exploring each stage of intellectual development, we will be focusing on six variables:

1. **Defining Feature-** This variable will describe what separates one thinking pattern from another. It will also provide a detailed description of each feature that reinforces its individuality and calls out what the variable is and is not.

2. **Principal Challenge-** The first and most prominent challenge that a thinker has to overcome to get to full critical thinking clarity. If there are any challenges in overcoming poor thinking, the principal challenge will define it.

3. **Knowledge of Thinking-** This variable will describe the level of self-awareness thinking capacity the thinker has. It will also measure the reflective awareness the thinker has when considering their own level of thinking. From complete unawareness to total clarity, this variable will attempt to diagnose where the thinker is on the scale.

4. **Skill in Thinking-** This variable will pinpoint where the thinker resides on the scale of thinking, from being completely unaware of their

thinking capabilities to overthinking. It will also describe how a thinker uses their understanding of the critical thinking process to think critically.

5. **Relevant Intellectual Traits-** This variable will elaborate on the fundamental intellectual trait that allows a thinker to think critically.

6. **Some Implications for Instruction-** This variable will describe the next steps to becoming a better critical thinker and what to do to start that journey.

This is by no means an exhaustive list, nor will it cover every question raised regarding the development, reliability, or validity of the stages. However, it will delve deeper into each one of these stages and provide a guideline for the proper execution of each developmental stage.

What is Critical Thinking?

The definition used in this book to base the premise of everything else we will be discussing is as follows:

The ability to improve one's critical thinking by implementing intellectual self-assessment systematically.

The reason it's essential to define this level of critical thinking is that people, in general, are critical thinkers. What we will be focusing on are those thinkers who use critical thinking in almost all categories of their lives (e.g., business life, personal life, family life, friendships, and law-abiding citizens).

We will not be referring to those thinkers who only use critical thinking in one area of their lives. The reason for this is that the level of a person's quality of life is determined by a multi-dimensional approach to their life and applying critical thinking to each area, not just in one area.

Assumptions

There are four assumptions made about critical thinking in this book:

1. Every person who develops as a critical thinker passes through predictable stages.
2. There is a required level of commitment that an individual must give to develop as a critical thinker to move on between each stage. This is a conscious effort and not automatic, so the thinker must make each of these steps intentional.
3. The intellectual quality of student learning is firmly connected to the success of the instruction the student receives.

4. When developing these skills, the possibility of regression is present.

Developing your thinking is a process that takes years, not weeks or months. It's hard work, and you can't shortcut your way around it by taking a course. This is a habit inducing a long-term journey. Here are the stages as we develop as thinkers.

Stage 1: The Unreflective Thinker
We have no idea or awareness that there are problems in our thinking.

Stage 2: The Challenged Thinker
We become aware of problems in our thinking, but we don't know what to do about it.

Stage 3: The Beginning Thinker
We implement some techniques to try to improve ourselves, but we don't do it consistently.

Stage 4: The Practicing Thinker
We realize that it's necessary to implement consistent habits if we want lasting change.

Stage 5: The Advanced Thinker
We get better the more we practice.

Stage 6: The Master Thinker
We are insightful, and our thinking becomes automatic.

Most people will live and die as unreflective thinkers never knowing that they have a problem much less how to fix it. It requires consistent daily practice and a commitment to establishing new habits to improve our thinking.

Critical Thinking Advantages

Critical thinking skills can prove highly valuable in the workplace, social situations, relationships, and your bank account. Being able to effectively problem solve is a lucrative skill the people would pay you for. But beyond that, it makes you a well-rounded person.

Approach. The type of approach to a problem varies from person to person. Being able to approach a problem the right way and solve it is what critical thinking prepares you to do. You can learn how to identify variables, approaches, and other factors to increase the likelihood of your success.

Saves time. When you're trained in critical thinking, you know which information you can immediately discard and which information is essential to hold onto. You have a clean filter from which to source in your effort to find the information you need. Critical thinking teaches you how to prioritize your time and resources by analyzing what's essential.

In appreciation of a variety of cultures and viewpoints. This is a direct effect of learning how to empathize with other people and their point of view. Critical thinking allows you to see the bigger picture without judgment and learn how to understand those things that are foreign to you. This makes for a well-rounded decision-making process. Empathy and understanding are critical to making good decisions.

More effective communication. By learning how to analyze and build evidence for anything, critical thinking can help make you a more effective communicator. Being able to convey relevant points to support your position is extremely valuable when communicating an idea or proposal adequately. When you know what you're talking about, though believe you.

Making decisions. Critical thinking allows you to make better decisions faster and a lot easier. You began to rely less on intuition or guessing and began to work based on the evidence and analytical results.

Reasoning. With critical thinking, you'll learn two types of reasoning-inductive and deductive-and when the appropriate time is to use each. Your decisions will be grounded in logic over emotion and rooted in evidence.

Stage One: The Unreflective Thinker

We are born unreflective thinkers. We don't know that thinking plays a role in our lives. We have no concept of it, and we don't notice that we are making assumptions based on the environment around us. We have no clue about how to analyze and assess our thinking, and we don't know how to determine our purposes or assumptions based on critical thinking.

Because we are unaware of it, we are not striving to improve it. Unfortunately, this causes a lot of problems in our lives, but we don't make the connection. We see what we believe as being true. We think that the decisions we make are solid. We don't have any kind of intellectual standards to follow, and we have no clue what those would look like if we had them.

We deceive ourselves in several ways while creating illusions to allow us to believe that we have a broader grasp of the bigger picture than we actually do. We walk around believing that we know more than what we do and that we are confident about what the world looks like to us. Will judge other people on their goodness or badness depending on how we perceive the world.

Our egocentric tendencies are in the forefront leading the way, but we don't realize it. We don't have the skills or the inclination to notice our self-centeredness and our prejudices. The bad news here is that unreflective thinkers go on to raise future unreflective thinkers. The cycle continues and goes on and on until someone questions their thinking. However, once you realize this, then you can move on to Stage II.

When you do that, you get closer to breaking the old bad habits of unreflective thinking. This is when we start to realize that there are some problems in our thinking that need to be corrected and that we realize we've been irrational in many ways and egocentric. When you reflect honestly, it leads to a healthy curiosity to change your thinking.

It's not enough just to see that you have problems with thinking, you also need to find out how to fix those. You might be able to articulate the problems you have, but nothing will change if you don't have the motivation to figure out the solutions.

Defining Feature: Unreflective thinkers, for the most part, don't know how thinking plays a part in their lives. More importantly, they don't realize the extent to which thinking is causing problems in their lives. Unreflective thinkers don't have the capability to step outside of themselves and assess their thinking so that they can improve it.

Knowledge of Thinking: Unreflective thinkers don't have the background knowledge to be able to think and take apart their thinking. High-quality thinking is required, and they don't have that. Nor do they have the ability to assess it or implement it accurately. Unreflective thinkers, for the most part, don't even know that thinking directly correlates to making assumptions, inferences, and implications in their point of view. They are utterly oblivious to all of these.

There are appropriate standards for the assessment of thinking. These are clarity, accuracy, precision, relevance, logicalness, etc. Unreflective thinkers have no concept that these standards exist.

Skills and thinking: Unreflective thinkers may have a variety of skills and thinking without being aware they have them. That is to say; they have no idea how they pick them up or even that they exist. As a result, these skills aren't implemented consistently because of the lack of awareness that they exist. The unreflective thinker will be easily misdirected based on their prejudices and misconceptions led by the quality of thought patterns.

Some implications for instruction: Unreflective thinkers can actually graduate from high school and college and still be completely unaware of their self their lack of self-reflecting and thinking. While it's true that most people do think, most people are unaware of how their thinking is structured in their heads or how to improve it. So when they run across problems in their thinking, they don't know how to identify or fix them.

Stage Two: The Challenged Thinker

If we don't know we have a problem we can't solve it. There is no way to fix something we don't know is broken. Without being aware of our own ignorance, we can't make the journey to find the knowledge we don't have. We need the skills to be able to obtain that knowledge.

As the unreflective thinker becomes aware, they move into the second stage of critical thinking. At this time, some things began to get noticed:

- We make assumptions that are questionable at the very least.

- We use misleading information and present it as fact.

- We imply things that are in direct conflict with the evidence we have.

- We failed to identify those implications in our thought process.

- We don't recognize the problems that we have.

- The concepts that we form are inaccurate.

- We take our prejudices to base our arguments around.

- We think irrationally and egocentrically.

When we become aware that our thinking is creating problems in our lives, then we move to the "challenged" stage. It dawns on us how dangerous our faulty thinking can be to our lives or the lives of others.

At this point in your thinking development, there is a genuine danger of deceiving yourself. Many people are resistant to accepting the thought that their thinking is an actual problem in their lives. Sometimes they'll go back to the unreflective stage. There's a lot of fear hiding around acknowledging where we actually are versus where we think we are.

You are not alone, however. The majority of people tend to defend themselves in their thinking. Many of us have never been taught how to think in school constructively. The absence of intellectual humility is quite prevalent among each different class of people of all ages and walks of life.

Active or passive resistance is the norm when it comes to challenging your own critical thinking. Most people reject the notion that they need to look inward to challenge their thinking. It's very important to be open to that process to move forward.

Defining features: These thinkers are just becoming aware that the role of thinking plays a part in their lives and that they're having problems because their thinking is mostly behind that.

Principal challenge: The challenged thinker's principal challenge is to become aware of how thinking affects their life and the underlying problems they experience as a result of their poor thinking.

Knowledge of Thinking: Challenged thinkers are starting to become aware that thinking is playing a part in the problems in their lives. On some level, they are beginning to realize that high-quality thinking requires reflective thinking and that that is something that is deliberate and not incidental. They understand that the thinking is often flawed, but they're not sure how to pick out and identify a lot of these flaws.

Challenged thinkers might be initially aware of thinking that involves standards for assessing thinking such as clarity, accuracy, precision, relevance, logicalness, etc., but they only have a beginner's grasp of the standards and minimal knowledge about what it would take to implement them into their thinking.

Challenged thinkers also become aware of the concept of self-deception in their thinking. This is also limited in its ability to understand this. The challenged thinker develops some reflective awareness of how thinking operates for good or bad.

Skill and thinking: for the most part, challenge thinkers have minimal ability when it comes to thinking. But in contrast to unreflective thinkers, challenge thinkers may have a variety of skills and think about being aware of them. As a consequence, many of the skills prevent them from developing their thinking further. This can cause them to inadvertently deceive themselves into believing that the thinking is more progressive than it really is. Of course, this makes it even harder for them to recognize problems in their poor-quality thinking. To overcome this, you should be able to gain insight into their poor thinking and apply intellectual skills across every facet of their lives.

Relevant intellectual trait: Intellectual humility is the primary intellectual trait at the stage for challenge thinkers. This allows them to see the problems as a result of their thinking.

Some implications for instruction: When teaching ourselves we have to understand that we do think and that our thinking also goes into left field. We have to purposefully leave discussions about thinking and get them consciously aware of how their thinking affects their lives. Model thinking is one example that can be used along with a practical application to help challenge thinkers intentionally think more critically.

Challenged thinkers need to be able to look at both low and high-quality thinking and compare and contrast those differences. Additionally, challenged thinkers have to compare the parts of thinking and the intellectual standards necessary to be able to assess their thinking. Also, challenged thinkers should be introduced to the idea of the awareness of our own ignorance in order to grasp the idea of intellectual humility.

Stage Three: The Beginning Thinker

 Once someone decides to develop their thinking skills, they move into the beginning thinker stage. This is where thinking is being taken seriously. New habits are trying to be formed and followed consistently. In this stage, there are a lot of realizations that come to light. It's a time for allowing these feelings to reveal themselves and not condemning them for existing. The key is to realize that you alone have the power to do something about it.

Once the realization hits that they are in a negative habit pattern of poor thinking, they have to be able to understand the nature of the problem. Egocentric thinking is sometimes common at this stage. We can notice how much we focus on our needs and forsake the needs of others. We may realize that rarely do we take into consideration other people's points of view over our own. We might even catch ourselves trying to persuade others to get what we want or give them and give them what they want so that we can also get what we want.

At this phase, we're just starting to:

- Assess situations and problems and their logic.
- Articulate specific questions.
- Verify information for relevance and accuracy in the situation.
- Determine between actual information and someone's perception of it.
- Separate and recognize assumptions that are guiding our inferences.
- Identify biased beliefs, misused inferences, and prejudices.
- Catch ourselves when we notice our interests are selfish and biased.

As beginning thinkers, we're starting to look at the different categories in our lives from a new perspective. We start realizing that our thinking in terms of clarity, accuracy, relevance, precision, and logicalness, plays a part in our overall critical thinking skills.

However, we haven't mastered it yet. We're still operating on a low level because it all feels weird to us. We have to force ourselves to stay disciplined and on track. We feel foolish starting from square one, and we don't like what we see when we're practicing.

To reach this stage of thinking, we have to shift our values. We have to explore how our thinking got to where it is and figure out why we think and believe as we do. This is accomplished by reflecting on who we are, where we were born, when we were born, who our parents are, and what associations we made growing up around friends and community.

If anyone of these factors were different, your belief system would be shaped differently than it is now. There are so many influences in your life that if any one of those was tweaked, it could give a completely different outcome. Knowing that we can start appreciating this fact and how little control we actually had over it. This can help when we're too hard on ourselves in certain areas to realize much of the control we think we have when we don't.

We have a lot of prejudices based on our culture, environment, family, and friends. Intentionally seeking out those flawed beliefs and replacing them with evidence-driven data can go a long way in helping us think critically.

Several modes of influence shape our minds. There are also different domains that help influence how we think:

- **Vocational:** we are influenced by our coworkers and our work environment.
- **Sociological:** we are influenced by social groups that we hang around.
- **Philosophical:** we allow our personal philosophies to influence our minds.
- **Ethical:** the way we define our obligations and how we behave as influenced by our minds.
- **Intellectual:** the ideas we have and influence our minds to play based on the ideas that we hold.
- **Anthropological:** cultural practices, taboos, and more influence our minds.
- **Ideological and political:** we are influenced by interest groups that surround us.
- **Economic:** the economic conditions that we live in influence our minds.
- **Historical:** history and the way we tell our stories to influence our minds.

- **Biological:** neurology and biology have a profound influence on our minds.
- **Theological:** our religious practices and attitudes surrounding that influence our minds.
- **Psychological:** our personality and personal psychology influence our minds.
- **Physiological:** our weight, height, and physical condition influence our minds.

When you look at it, we don't know very much about our minds. Our inner mind does a lot of heavy lifting for us. It decides whether we're joyous or frustrated. It limits what we can see and what we can imagine. It can also provide some peace. If we make friends with our minds, we give it the motivation to step into the role of a leader in our thinking.

Defining feature: the beginning thinker is actively working to take control of their thinking across all areas of their lives. They realize and acknowledge they have fundamental problems with their thinking and make the first steps to try to understand how they can take control and make improvements. Although they try to take the steps, they have limited insight into the extent to which their thinking is troubled. As a result, they don't have a plan for how to improve their thinking, so most of the time they are firing on trial and error.

Principal challenge: the most challenging part is for them to see how important it is for them to develop as a thinker. They will try to find ways to improve themselves as a thinker and fully commit to that goal.

Knowledge of thinking: beginning thinkers are starting to understand the concepts of assumptions, inferences, implications, a point of view, etc., that play a role in their thinking. They do recognize there is a specific set of standards for assessing thinking like clarity, accuracy, precision, relevance, logicalness, etc., but they also realize that they have to take them into themselves and intentionally use them when thinking. They are at a beginner level of comprehending the role of egocentric thinking.

Skill and thinking: beginning thinkers are more receptive to being critiqued about their thought powers. They have enough skill to start supervising their own thoughts, but they are often inconsistent.

Relevant intellectual traits: the primary intellectual trait that's needed in this phase is a form of intellectual humility. This allows them to recognize the problems in their thinking. They also have to have some level of intellectual confidence when it comes to reasoning because that's a trait that allows them to accept the challenge and begin developing as a critical thinker despite the fact that they have a shallow understanding of what it means to perform high-quality reasoning. Beginner thinkers have enough perseverance to combat thinking problems, but they still lack a clear solution to those problems. They are more aware of the problems than there are solutions for them.

Some implications for instruction: once a thinker is convinced that the thinking is not monitored or controlled then they're able to improve. When they realize that good thinking practice leads to automatic critical thinking, they have more success reaching that goal. All of us need to develop good habits of thinking and that requires consistent practice.

Stage Four: The Practicing Thinker

A person becomes a practicing thinker once they recognize and embrace that improvement thinking requires consistent practice and adopts the habits of regular practice. There are several ways to go about this process. The problem with this is that most people don't follow through. They get discouraged and give up too soon. This requires a commitment to see the practice through to the end and to develop a realistic plan that will work out long-term. Something that will fit in with your lifestyle and is easily adaptable into a habit.

It is not unusual to try different methods at this stage to see what works right for you. The main point is to be realistic about what you can do consistently every day and to experiment with several plans before you settle on one. Protect yourself from getting discouraged. Make a decision right now that no matter what happens you're not going to allow discouragement to derail your efforts from consistent practice. This is a process and not something that you can achieve overnight.

Defining feature: at this stage, practicing thinkers realize they have habits that need to be developed to improve their thinking. They recognize that problems exist in their thinking and they know that they need a system to be able to address them. They have gotten in the habit of analyzing their thinking in several ways because they realize the importance of practicing consistently. However, they're still new to this, especially how to approach it in an organized way, so they still have a limited understanding of the deeper levels of their thinking.

Principal challenge: practicing thinkers need to concentrate on cultivating their awareness of the need to be consistent when practicing their thinking.

Knowledge of thinking: practicing thinkers are farther along on the scale compared to beginning thinkers in that they become they acquire more knowledge of what it actually takes to monitor their thinking in terms of concepts, assumptions, inferences, implications, points of view, etc. Practicing thinkers also begin to understand what it takes to assess their thinking for clarity, accuracy, precision, relevance, logicalness, etc. They realize they need a system for critical thinking and for internalizing their habits that are going to get them better at that thinking. They also understand that there is a natural tendency of the mind to engage in self-deception and egocentric thinking.

Skill and thinking: practicing thinkers can critique their plan for initializing practice because they have enough of the skill to be able to do that. They can also formulate a realistic self-reflection of their own powers of thought. Practicing thinkers also can regularly monitor or supervise their thoughts. They're able to see the strengths and weaknesses in their thinking accurately. They can also recognize their own egocentric thinking and the egocentric thinking of others. Not only that, but they are also in the habit of monitoring their thinking, even though sometimes they're not very successful at it.

Relevant intellectual traits: the primary intellectual trait that a practicing thinker has is intellectual perseverance. This allows them to develop a realistic plan for implementing system thinking practice. Practicing thinkers at this level can incite intellectual humility which is required to realize and evaluate the thinking in all levels of their lives and that it also should be subjected to critiques.

Some implications for instruction: there are specific, predictable structures of thought that as humans we need to learn to understand that is a must. Thinking is powered by questions that we want the answers to. We need information to get those questions answered. We have to interpret the information we're given to be able to implement the thinking critically. At this point, practicing thinkers should be developing the habits whenever there's trying to figure something out. They'll begin to see that there are connections between the various subject matters that their learning.

Stage Five: The Advanced Thinker

Defining Feature: Good habits have been established by thinkers at this level. Their deeper thought levels also have much more insight and analytic skills when looking at the different categories of their lives. However, advanced thinkers aren't yet able to attain high-level thinking across all of these categories. They have their egocentric nature well in hand and consistently make an effort to think in fair-minded terms, but can fall back into egocentrism and have a one-sided perspective.

Principal challenge: The challenge for advanced thinkers is to develop a deeper insight into problems of thought and to understand the need for consistent thinking practice implementation.

Knowledge of thinking: Active thinkers have consistent monitoring of thinking concepts well in hand. They have an abundance of knowledge in this regard. Advanced thinkers are also competent in what is necessary to analyze their thinking for clarity, accuracy, precision, logicalness, relevance, etc. They appreciate their ability to deep dive into their critical thinking and implement those habits daily. They know how important thinking plays a part in their lives. They understand they can control the power that egocentrism plays in their lives and their thinking.

Skill in thinking: Advanced thinkers take the initiative to improve their plan for practice thinking continuously. They continually evaluate their thoughts and can identify strategies to help them reduce their egocentric thoughts.

Relevant intellectual traits: High-level intellectual humility is required at this stage. This allows the thinker to recognize egocentric thoughts in their own lives, as well as prejudicial and arrogant thoughts.

Implications for instruction: it's essential to know the criteria for becoming an advanced thinker and that it's perceived this goal is essential. We must foster the awareness of egocentrism and sociocentrism in thinking by seeing oneself in the topic.

Stage Six: The Accomplished Thinker

Defining feature: accomplished thinkers take control of their thinking, and they're also continually analyzing that thinking to improve strategies for better thinking skills and methods. They have the basics down, so critical thinking for them is intuitive and purposeful. Regularly, they rise to the level of conscious awareness through consistent practice and are good at analyzing their thinking across all categories in their lives as well as developing new ways to look at problems and use their critical thinking to solve them. Accomplished thinkers are very committed to being fair in their thinking process, and they have a stronghold over there egocentric nature.

Principal challenge: to get to the point where they're reaching the highest levels of critical thinking in every category of their life.

Knowledge of thinking: accomplished thinkers actively engage in analyzing the role in their thinking when considering concepts, inferences, implications, points of view, etc., but are also consistently improving. Accomplished thinkers have a high degree of knowledge and insight. They assess their own thinking to find clarity, accuracy, precision, relevance, logicalness, etc. Accomplished thinkers have strong habits in their process of thinking. They understand how sociocentrism can egocentric roles play in their thinking as well as in human beings as a whole.

Skill in thinking: accomplished thinkers often critique their thinking in their lives and are always looking to improve. They're always aware of their thoughts and insightfulness and can convey those strengths and weaknesses about their thinking. They realize that as humans they are fallible, but they're continually looking to improve in every area of their lives. Others are drawn to them because they appreciate their thinking as it relates to complicated issues.

Relevant intellectual traits:
accomplished thinkers are high in
intellectual humility, intellectual
perseverance, intellectual integrity,
intellectual courage, intellectual
empathy, intellectual autonomy
intellectual responsibility, and fair-
mindedness. The accomplished thinker
integrates the fundamental values,
beliefs, desires, emotions, and actions
in their thinking.

Some implications for instruction:
most of us are generally not very
accomplished thinkers. But it's important
to learn what it takes to become an
accomplished thinker. It's important to
see it as possible, so long as practicing
habits are formed.

General implications for instruction:
human beings will be oblivious to the
concept of thinking unless they're
challenged to look at it. Whether that's
through instruction or education,
intellectual vocabularies must be
established and presented to the

thinker, so they can start questioning their systems and processes.

Discovering The Parts Of Thinking

Humans have to realize that they have to use some aspects because without them their thinking would be unintelligible. Thinking is often prompted by the questions we ask ourselves. Those questions are driven by some sort of purpose.

In order to answer these questions, we have to get the information that is relevant based on how we interpret it. This is called inferences. Inferences are based on things we assume and require that we use familiar concepts to organize the information in a way to form that inference.

Thinking begins intellectually and then moves forward into implications and consequences. So whenever we try to figure out a problem, it's a good idea to take command of the structures: purpose, information, inferences, assumptions, concepts, point of view, and implications.

By taking command of this, we take command of our own thinking, and we provide a way to allow us to think critically in the context of our lives. So basically to become a good thinker, we need to be able to figure things out using clues we find around us.

An excellent way to start understanding how to create proper thinking is to understand that everything around us is for a purpose. It's our job to connect how we organize to figure these things out. Once you understand the purpose of these things, then you can learn from them and build off of them until you get a bigger picture. We also learned that we have to ask questions to gain a broader picture for us to draw from it.

The Advantages Of Critical Thinking

The good news is that when we embrace critical thinking, we can do a lot of things. Some of those include:

- Explaining goals and purposes
- Clarify questions that we need answers to any problems we need to resolve
- Organize and gather information and data
- Assess the meaning and significance of information given to us
- Demonstrate that we understand concepts
- Identify assumptions
- Consider the implications and consequences

- Examine things from more than one point of view
- Be able to state what is said clearly and accurately
- Test and verify for accuracy
- Stay on task and thinking and not wander off on other thoughts
- Express ourselves precisely the way we want to
- Deal with severe problems and issues
- Be able to consider other people's perspectives
- Express logical thinking
- Tell the difference between necessary and unimportant matters

Once we are instructed on how to do these things, we can learn content on a deeper level and have it become a permanent part of our thinking process.

- We are also better able to explain this to others and apply what we've learned.
- We are better able to connect what we're learning in one

category to another and how it relates to the big picture.

- We can also ask better questions.
- We can understand materials like textbooks and other documents better.
- We can understand the instructions better.
- We can understand what other people are talking about.
- We can write better.
- We can apply more of what we're learning to our everyday lives.
- We become more motivated to learn.
- It becomes easier for us to be taught.

Chapter 2: Mental Toughness and The Elemental Structures of Thinking

Elemental Structures:

To become an advanced thinker, we must learn how to analyze our thinking. That comes from identifying and questioning its elemental structures. The elemental structures are:

1. **Clarity:** The ability to understand the meaning.
    Questions to ask-
        - Could you elaborate further?

- Could you give me an example?
- Could you illustrate what you mean?

2. **Accuracy:** Free from distortions or mistakes.

   Questions to ask-
   - How could we check on that?
   - How could we find out if that is true?
   - How could we test or verify that?

3. **Precision:** Accurate to the required level of detail.

   Questions to ask-
   - Could you be more specific?
   - Could you give me

more
details?
- Could you be
  more exact?

4. **Relevance:** Relating to the
   situation at present.
   Questions to ask-
   - How does
     that relate to
     the problem?
   - How does
     that bear on
     the
     question?
   - How does
     that help us
     with the
     issue?

5. **Depth:** Having multiple
   interrelationships and
   complexities.
   Questions to ask-
   - What factors
     make this a
     tough
     problem?

- What are some of the complexities of this question?
- What are some of the complications we need to deal with?

6. **Breadth:** Containing more than one viewpoint.

    Questions to ask-
    - Do we need to look at this from another viewpoint?
    - Do we need to consider another point of view?
    - Do we need to look at this in other ways?

7. **Logic:** No contradictions; everything makes sense.

Questions to ask-

- Does all this make sense together?
- Does your first paragraph fit in with your last?
- Does what you say follow the evidence?

8. **Significance:** Ignoring the trivial and focusing on the important.

Questions to ask-

- Is this the most significant problem to consider?
- Is this the central idea to focus on?
- Which of these facts are the most important?

9. **Fairness:** Not one-sided; justifiable.

Questions to ask-

- Do I have any vested interest in this matter?
- Am I sympathetically representing the viewpoints of others?

Elements of Thought

Take into consideration the different elements of thought and how each contributes to improved critical thinking skills.

Point of View:
This is your vantage point; the place where you view your world from. This includes your perception of the environment around you. It's important to understand that your viewpoint has limits and to consider the viewpoints of others.

1. Recognize your point of view.

2. Find other viewpoints other than my own and analyze their strengths and weaknesses.
3. Try to maintain a level of fair-mindedness when analyzing all viewpoints.

Questions to consider when checking your point of view:

- Can I see this situation differently? What other ways can I look at this situation?
- What am I focused on? What do I think about what I'm focused on?
- Are there other reasonable views other than my own? What are they? What does my point of view overlook?
- How do people of other cultures view this?
- In any given situation, which viewpoints make the most sense?
- Do I have a hard time putting myself into different viewpoints that I disagree with?
- What's the author's point of view?

- Do I challenge myself by analyzing viewpoints other than my own?

Purpose:

Your purpose is what you're trying to achieve. It's your goal, your ultimate end game. You want to make sure that you are absolutely clear about your purpose and how to get there.

1, State your purpose with clarity.

2. Differentiate your related purposes from your primary purpose.

3. Continue to stay aligned with your intended target.

Questions to ask yourself about your purpose:

- My purpose in doing _____ is what?
- What is the goal of this task/assignment/job?
- Is it time to revise our purpose?
- What is the purpose of this action?
- What is your primary goal in this thought process?

Information:

Information does not necessarily mean that it is correct or accurate. Instead, it is defined as experiences, facts, and data we use to make decisions.

1. Use the data you have to support your claims.
2. Balance your information by finding the pros and cons of your position.
3. All information should be clear, relevant, and accurate.
4. Gather enough information to use for your purposes.

Questions to ask yourself about information:

- To answer this question, what information do I need?
- Depending on the problem, what data do I need to solve it?
- Should I accumulate more information?

- Taking the purpose and goal into consideration, what information pertains to these?
- What information do I have that supports my claim?
- How do I know the information I have is correct and accurate?
- Is there any other information I need to collect?

Interpretation and Inference:
When the mind tries to figure something out it's called inferring. There shouldn't be any inferences outside of what evidence is provided in the situation. When you reach a conclusion, that's called an inference. Inferences use evidence and come as a result of evaluating that evidence.

1. Only infer what the evidence presents to you.
2. Inferences should be consistent with each other.
3. Underneath inferences are assumptions. You should be able to identify them.

Questions to ask yourself about inferences:

- What conclusions am I drawing?
- Does my inference make logical sense?
- Are there conclusions I haven't considered that I need to?
- Does my conclusion draw from my data?
- My reasoning is based on what?
- Is it possible that there is another conclusion that can be reached?
- What is the best conclusion given all the facts?
- How should the data be interpreted?

Concepts:

Concepts are principles, ideas, or theories we use to try to have things make sense to us. Concepts and ideas shape all reasoning.

1. Explain key concepts clearly.
2. Entertain the option of different definitions of concepts.
3. Use precision when using concepts.

Questions to ask yourself about concepts:

- Is the idea I'm using in my thinking causing problems for myself or anyone else?
- How can I explain a good theory better?
- Which hypothesis is my reasoning using?
- What relevant points should I draw when reasoning through this problem?
- What type of thinking is the author using? Is there anything wrong with it?

Question the issue:

Our thinking is guided by the questions we ask. The more specific our questions, the more clarity we gain. The question's job is to guide our thinking, so it should be obvious.

1. Precisely and clearly state the question.

2. Ask a variation of the same question several times to clarify its meaning.
3. Break down the question into sub-questions.
4. Separate clearly defined questions from vague questions.

Questions to ask yourself about questions:

- What's the question I need to answer?
- Is there a better way to frame the question?
- Is this question crystal clear and/or complicated?

Assumptions:

Assumptions are automatic beliefs you take for granted. You can have them on a conscious or subconscious level. Your assumptions should be backed up by strong evidence to support it.

Assumptions are based on reasoning.

1. Determine whether your assumptions are justifiable and clearly define what they are.
2. Take into consideration how your point of view is shaped by assumptions.

Questions to ask yourself about assumptions:
- What am I taking for granted?
- Is there something I'm assuming that I shouldn't?
- What assumption leads to this conclusion?
- What are some important assumptions I've been making?

Implications and Consequences:
Claims/truths that follow in a logical procession from other claims/truths.
They follow from thoughts.
Consequences follow from actions.

Let's talk about mental toughness:

We understand the world in different ways. How we take in information not only shapes what we think and believe, but also shapes the perceptions we have in our environment. Several mental models explain this complex subject, and we're going to explore some of them right now.

Keep in mind that a mental model is like a map that summarizes how something works. The more models you have to draw from, the bigger your resources become, and the more likely you are to be able to pick and choose the ones you need when it really matters. When you're trying to improve your critical thinking skills, having a surplus of different techniques to choose from is invaluable.

The type of mental model we use is based on who we are as a person and what we do in life. For example, a scientist thinks in terms of logic and testing, so the type of mental models that would be most useful to that person would be models that reinforce that type of thinking.

There is no wrong answer when you're choosing mental models, it's merely a matter of preference and based on a person's experience. However, learning more models in different areas makes for a well-rounded person. So the more models that you can be exposed to the broader your toolbox becomes.

Mental models aren't useful unless you have the foundation to put them on. If they don't work together in some sort of pattern or logical concept, they aren't going to be used in everyday life. These models need to be incorporated into your thinking, and they also have to be accessible to you within your present environment. Trying to remember facts and recall isn't enough. You have to have an anchor to hang these experiences and models on.

Here are several mental models that we summarized for you. This will give you a basic overview of the mental models available out there so that you can pick and choose which ones you find most relevant to you and do further research on them.

https://www.criticalthinking.org/ctmodel/logic-model1.htm

Mental Models:

Thinking concepts

The map is not the territory.

Maps are imperfect. They're only a representation of reality, not the actual reality. Maps are a sample of a particular period in time representing something that used to exist but no longer does. When we are thinking through problems and trying to solve them to make better choices, it's important to keep this in mind.

Circle of competence

We get blind spots in revision when we allow our ego in the driver's seat. It's our competence that should be driving our ego. We must have a good understanding of our strengths so that we know when we have a leading edge over other people. If you can be honest with yourself about what you don't know and where you're most vulnerable and how to improve, that's when you can increase your competence and decision-making, thus yielding better outcomes.

First Principles Thinking

This is sometimes called "reasoning from first principles." It's a useful tool that helps bring clarity to difficult problems by dissecting the ideas and facts from any assumptions made based on them. This is one of the leading ways to reverse engineer difficult situations and yield creativity. When you can strip away the problems and dissect them like this, you'll find only the core essentials that are left. To produce something new and build your knowledge around that, you have to know the first principles of something.

An example of this would be the differences between a chef and a cook. A chef invents his or her own recipes. They know their ingredients and how they'll work together. On the other hand, the cook using analogy follows the recipes and merely assembles something that's already been created.

When reasoning from first principles and reasoning by analogy is that if the cook didn't have the recipe, they wouldn't be able to produce the meal. However, the chef has real knowledge about each ingredient and how they work together, so he could recreate it at will.

https://fs.blog/2018/04/first-principles/

Thought Experiments

Sometimes called "devices of the imagination used to investigate the nature of things," thought experiments are used in disciplines like philosophy and physics to examine the factors that are known to us. By doing that, it reveals new pathways for asking new questions and exploring various paths. These are incredibly effective because they allow us to learn from mistakes and see future ones down the road so we can bypass them. It equips us to tackle the potential consequences of our actions and examine history to make better decisions. They also can help us figure out the best way to get where we want to go and decide which direction.

Second-order Thinking

Most people can see before it happens the consequences of their actions. This is first-order thinking and is usually pretty easy to do to make sure you get the same results that other people get. Second-order thinking is the ability to think further down the road and think big picture. We have to consider our actions and their immediate consequences, but we also have to think about the effects that those actions will have down the road. If we don't think about these things, it can lead to serious negative consequences.

Probabilistic Thinking

Think of the word "probability." Probabilistic thinking is the act of trying to use math and logic to estimate how likely any outcome will happen. If we're talking about improving the accuracy of our decisions, it's one of the best tools we have. Every single moment of our lives springs from an infinitely complex set of factors. Probabilistic thinking allows us to select the most probable outcomes.

Fat-tailed processes are included in this.

A fat tail can be disguised as a normal distribution. That's because outlier events are more likely to occur than in a normal distribution. It takes on the shape of a large "tail." If the fat tail is on the negative side, the risk can be higher. However, if the fat tail is on the positive side, it can be more profitable. Most of the world we socialize and is regarded as fat-tailed rather than normally distributed.

Bayesian Updating

This is the process of taking into account all probabilities and then updating them as new information reveals itself. This method is named after Thomas Bayes. Our intuitive decision-making process is not necessarily behind this method. Instead, we have to use prior information combined with new information to come up with the best decisions in this model. It's considered very constructive and used often.

Inversion

Inversion assists you in identifying and removing challenges in your path to success. The root word "invert," means to turn upside down. So taking that into consideration, it means that you put yourself on the opposite end of the situation and look at it from that perspective. Most people are used to looking at a problem from one angle. Inversion enables you to turn the problem around and look at it from the other side. Most of us start at the beginning and work from there; sometimes it can be way more useful to start at the end first.

Occam's Razor

Occam's razor explains that the simplest explanation is likely to be the answer. It supposes that you can make more confident decisions by basing your information on the factors that have the fewest moving parts. That's great news if you're currently consuming all of your energy trying to disprove complicated scenarios. Occam's razor suggests that the most straightforward answer is usually the right one.

Hanlon's Razor

Hanlon's Razor states that the explanation with the least amount of intent is most likely the correct one. This model forces us to ask ourselves if there is another reasonable explanation for why something has happened. It's a great reminder to us that people make mistakes. To look for options instead of picking out missed chances, we should not assume that poor results are the fault of a person's poor choices. This model helps us avoid idealizing situations and assuming ourselves with paranoia that is unfounded. Basically, Hanlon's Razor states that we should not label a person with the intent of malice that is more accurately explained away by stupidity.

Systems

Scale

Systems are sensitive to scale. Behaviors tend to change when moving the scale up or down. Rough quantification has to be applied to the scale that we are predicting the system. When we are studying complicated systems, we must always estimate the scale that we are watching, evaluating, or predicting the system.

For example, in the higher education arena, the purpose is to equip graduates with the tools to enable them to tackle complicated, correlative problems. That means they need the flexibility to work on problems. The scale of those problems, whether minute or massive, determines the response by the graduate. So if a graduate has a degree in liberal arts but finds no jobs hiring for that type of degree/industry, he has to adjust his behavior/skill set to jobs he is eligible for in his industry.

Another example would be a teacher addressing behavioral issues in the classroom. The scale at which the teacher must meet the consequence of actions is determined by the offense. If little Johnny is distracting the class by talking to other students, then perhaps the teacher would give him lunch detention. But if little Johnny decided to throw a chair across the room, the scale of the punishment would move up in accordance with the scale of the offense.

https://www.sciencedirect.com/science/article/pii/S1871187117302511

Law Of Diminishing Returns

This law states that there is eventually a decrease in the value of something. We can relate this to most real-world scenarios. There are many situations in which the law of diminishing returns becomes negative. For example, a sick person who has an infection and is given antibiotics will soon no longer have an infection. There is a point at which giving them more antibiotics will not improve their situation. At some point, there is a diminishing return on the medical care given.

Pareto Principle

This principle states that a small portion is responsible for the most significant effect. For example, 20% of the population brings in 80% of the nation's wealth. This principle can be applied to various situations from money to population. The Pareto Principle was named after an Italian Vilfredo Pareto after he observed that 80% of Italy's land was owned by 20% of its population.

Feedback Loops

An outside force is static to change in a feedback loop unless it's automatic. All complicated systems are exposed to a positive and negative feedback loop where point A causes point B, which in turn affects point A and C, and so on, and so on. To get point A back into line, an opposite change in Points A and B has to occur to maintain the balance of the whole system. An example of this would be the human body temperature.

The Butterfly Effect

The slightest changes in conditions have a significant effect on future outcomes and ripple forever. This means that elements in our world and the decisions that humans make are unpredictable.

For example, if you were to go back in time and assassinate Hitler as a child, you would set in motion an alternate set of events that send a ripple through time. Everything we know to be true would be altered. The ripples get larger the longer they are allowed to flow. Even the tiniest change can yield major changes.

Preferential Attachment (Cumulative Advantage)

The status of the leader is preserved by giving the current leader or ruler more of the prize than any of the others. An excellent example of this would be a company that has ten times the customers as the second-largest company will have a preferential attachment dynamic.

Emergence

Low-order factors serve as the foundation for high-level behavior to emerge. This yields an exponential result. Emergent behavior cannot be predicted by studying each part alone.

Irreducibility

There's a certain point where you cannot reduce a processor system to get a particular result. There is an irreducible level, and below that, the result desired cannot happen. For example, trying to build an entire vehicle using only one part is impossible. At a certain point, a result becomes irreducible.

The tragedy of the Commons

A resource that is not preserved by an individual responsible for its preservation will be depleted over time.

This concept was first introduced by Garrett Hardin, an economist, and ecologist.

The fear of missing out causes an accelerated rate of depleting the resource if each individual yields more personal benefit than the cost incurred unless people collaborate.

Gresham's Law

In an environment where currency is circulated, the forged currency will drive out real currency. This is because the real currency is held onto while the forged currency is used in the market. Another parallel to draw is good and bad behavior in humans. Bad behavior will drive out good behavior in a system that is morally bankrupt. When speaking on the economy, bad practices will drive out good practices. To keep the balance, regulation, and oversight are required to prevent falling into Gresham's Law. Financier Thomas

Gresham is the namesake for Gresham's Law.

Algorithms

An algorithm is like a map with a set of instructions leading to a destination or outcome. Usually, you can recognize it in its "If → then" statements. Algorithms are used in social media sites like Facebook and YouTube. It's the blueprint that leads you to the outcome you want.

Fragility – Robustness – Antifragility

Fragility, robustness, and antifragility is a sliding scale. It's relevant to how responsive a system is to variability that is negative. The negative variability has a disproportionately negative impact.

Think about a ceramic cup that shatters from a 7-foot fall, but stays intact, or receives drastically less damage at a two-foot fall.

However, if a ceramic cup got stronger when dropped, then it would be labeled as antifragile.

Redundancy

The concept behind redundancy is to never assume or rely solely on the individual components of any system. Redundancy built into the system allows the integrity of the total system to be preserved. Without such a fail-safe effort, systems tend to disintegrate over time.

Margin of Safety

The margin of safety is similar to redundancy in the sense that a margin for error is built into a system. When an elevator is constructed, it has a weight limit that's usually more than a realistic scenario in which its riders would be unlikely to reach. So giving a margin of safety is seen as intelligent and a way to avoid tragedy.

Criticality

The process of a system transitioning from one phase to another results in the system becoming critical. Before the phase changes, the unit before the new phase is higher than the next unit. The term "critical mass" means the mass required to have a critical event occur. An example of this would be the inner workings of the nuclear system.

Network Effects

For a network to be a network, it has to be comprised of several smaller elements that connect. A great example is the telephone network. One telephone is useless, but if everyone has a telephone, then the network becomes very valuable and can work as intended.

Via Negativa

Doctors implement a form of via negativa when they take another to "First, do no harm." When bad elements are removed as opposed to adding the right elements, this is called via negativa. For example, when one student in a classroom is disrupting the class, it's more useful to remove that student rather than punish the entire class.

The Lindy Effect

The current lifespan of an object is related to its expected lifespan; This is called the Lindy Effect. An example would be classic literature. If Jane Austen's works have been read for 100 years, it's expected that they will be read for another 100 years. This only applies to non-perishable objects or ideas. A human wouldn't be expected to live 50 more years if they lived to be 50.

Renormalization Group

This technique tries to renormalize a group after a small group of unrepentant individuals influences those around them on a larger scale. This idea has its origins in physics. The application of this technique tries to explain why this strange dynamic happens.

Spring-loading

In an unpredictable world, it's essential to protect ourselves against adverse events by engaging in positively spring-loaded relationships. The opposite can be devastating. For a system to be spring-loaded, it has to be coiled in either a positive or negative direction.

As long as the user does something to keep it active, a spring-loaded mode will persist. For example, if a user holds down a mouse button the state will continue to exist. However, if the user releases the button, the system closes the state it's in.

Complex Adaptive Systems

A complex adaptive system can understand itself and change based on that self-awareness. This is different from a general complex system. These are social systems. Complex adaptive systems are unpredictable and cannot be influenced. For example, the stock market may change based on events or opinions, but a hurricane does not stop becoming a hurricane based on the opinions of the weather forecaster.

Military and war

The Front Lines

This method doesn't rely on advisors, data, and reports without first seeing the front lines for himself. Those things can be riddled with mistakes or biases. Generally, leaders can benefit in almost every situation from seeing the front because it allows them to see the information firsthand and make decisions accordingly.

Asymmetric Warfare

In the asymmetry model, one side appears to "play by different roles" than the other side due to the specific circumstances they find themselves in. This model is usually used when one side has limited resources, and they're looking for a quick insurgency. They can't overpower their opponents with muscle, so they use other tactics. Terrorism is one example of this model.

Two-Front War

This can be a useful tactic when trying to squash internal disgruntlement so they can focus on the competition. In World War II, Russia and Germany became enemies. As a result, Germany had to divide its troops and send them to two separate fronts which made them weaker on both fronts than if they had stayed one troop.

Counterinsurgency

If asymmetric insurgent warfare is used for a prolonged period of time, competitors have a chance to develop counterinsurgency strategies. A feedback loop can be created when each side falls leads between insurgency and counterinsurgency.

Mutually Assured Destruction

This concept states that the stronger that two competitors become, the less likely they are to destroy one another. The most prominent example of this is the nuclear arms race in the 20th century. In business, it can be displayed as the avoidance of damaging price wars between competitors. Sometimes though, and a fat-tailed scenario, the possibility that mutually specific destruction scenarios are reality can make them more severe if one side makes a mistake.

The "Why" Model

The premise is that to inspire action we need to make sure our message is communicated in an obvious precise manner. As such, when we move forward, we need to lead with the question "why."

Asking this question gets her brain turning and producing a series of questions that will only draw closer to their awareness, therefore, reinforcing their sense of inner purpose. The "why" becomes the front door to justifying our reason. When we know our "why," were no longer aimlessly wandering about. We have direction and are ready and prepared to take action.

The power of the "why" question has been used for centuries to motivate individuals to take action and stir up crowds. The "why model" is one of the most useful techniques and sales to grab the customer's attention. When providing customers with their why they're more likely to invest in the solution to their problems, however, to get to that point, a salesman has to employ the "why" model.

Asking the right "why" questions and being able to handle the psychological reasons that spark a sale successfully, is the reason why the model works. It's also a great tool when trying to determine personal meaning. Counselors try to help people get to the bottom of their pain by helping them raise self-awareness through the "why" model.

Pavlovian Association

More than likely you've heard of Pavlov's dog at least once in your life. It's one of these terms that's thrown around to discuss conditioning techniques. Classical conditioning is a keyword that talks about the biological stimulus being introduced, while combined with a neutral stimulus like a bell to help form the learning process. In this case, the subject was a dog. When the dog makes the association between food and the bell it will elicit the same response during the then neutral stimulus, the same as it would during the biological stimulus.

When Pavlov's dog came across food, it started to salivate. Eventually, it would salivate just by listening to the sound of the bell.

This was a huge discovery. It opened the dog training realm and helped teach more dog-friendly approaches to training. It also was a potent psychological tool that could be applied to anyone of us.

We all have been victims of the Pavlovian Association whether consciously or subconsciously. Just look at commercials, for example. Products pay a lot of money to be associated with popular events and celebrities because they know you can't help but associate with your favorites.

Most of the work is done in the subconscious, so any conscious attempt to avoid it is usually pointless. It's a beautiful mental model for the influence of others as well as self-awareness.

Bias From Over Influence By Authority

This is an imperative mental model. Authority is an exciting concept that has been famous throughout history. The idea of authority is approached from numerous angles. Nazi Germany and communist Russia help people come to terms with the fact that authoritarian regimes are not the best path for any social group.

Every human relationship dynamic is a power-play for authority over other people. It's something that's inside all of us. Awareness that it exists is the first step in learning to control it before it gets out of hand.

Bias from being over-influenced by authority is learned early on. As long as the person pledges their allegiance to the authoritarian figure, the bias stays in place. Authority may give temporary security, but this is a mirage that rarely lasts long term. Bias by the authority if treated with bad intentions, can instigate bad events in motion if people don't recognize the power it has and the effect on their own decision-making.

Entropy

Entropy can be used in a lot of different disciplines and for many different reasons. Some examples include thermodynamics, entropy and information theory, entropy and cosmology, and entropy in statistical mechanics. The word entropy gets its name from the Greek word entropy "turning toward." It was invented by German physicist Rudolf Clausius in 1865. He was trying to measure the level of disorder within a system. The system referred to thermodynamics has been used to explain the change in randomness in any system.

When entropy is high, randomness is high with an assistant and vice versa.

The more complexity we bring, the more we increase entropy. There's no use in trying to control entropy because it will keep increasing over time.

https://thequintessentialmind.com/mental-models/

Laws Of Thermodynamics

This describes energy in a closed system. Useful energy is continuously being lost, and energy cannot be created or destroyed. Applying this lesson to the social world can be profitable when you're talking about business.

Reciprocity

This tells us that if I push on the wall, the wall pushes back with equal force. When we're talking about biology, if one individual acts on another, the action will be reciprocated in kind.

Velocity

Velocity and speed are two different things. Velocity speed plus factor: or how fast something gets to a destination. If an object moves forward and backward it's not showing velocity. Velocity plus the addition of the vector is what we should use in everyday life.

Relativity

Physics is where you hear the concept of relativity, but taking from that idea that an observer cannot understand the system if he's part of it. For example, traveling in a car going 80 mph does not feel like he's moving, but an outside observer can see that the vehicle is moving.

Activation energy

A chemical reaction requires the input of a critical level of activation energy to get the reaction going. Combustible elements by themselves are not enough to start this chain reaction.

Catalysts

The catalyst maintains a chemical reaction or starts it, but isn't itself or reactant. The reaction may slow down or stop altogether without the addition of catalysts. In a social system, any of these traits are similar.

Leverage

Exerting a small output of force yields a high output of force through leverage. It's the understanding that we can apply this to the practical world that can be a source of great joy and success.

Inertia

An object in motion will stay in motion unless acted upon by an outside force. This is one of the physical principles of motion, but individuals can display the same behavior.

Alloying

Alloying involves mixing different elements to form new substances, which is not a novel concept. However, the process of alloying demonstrates that combining two elements can result in properties that are more than just the sum of the individual parts—for example, the resulting alloy can be significantly stronger. This enhanced strength enables the creation of larger physical structures. Similarly, these principles of combination and synergy can be applied in social contexts to yield enhanced outcomes.

Viscosity

Viscosity is the measure of how hard it is for one layer of fluid to slide over another layer. The lesson in this is that we change the scale we change what forces are relevant.

The Biological World

Incentives

Creatures and humans respond to incentives to prosper. A steady stream of incentives tends to cause a person to have consistent behavior, to a point. Humans are a pretty great example of this, as we are driven by money, pleasure, and the need to avoid pain.

Adaptation

Humans tend to adapt to their surroundings to survive, which is a combination of their environment and genetics. These are not passed on genetically, but as a way to adapt to the exterior world.

Evolution By Natural Selection

Charles Darwin and Alfred Russel Wallace both realized that species evolve through random mutation and different survival rates. This led to the belief that nature decides who survives and who doesn't.

Replication

In biology, the fundamental building block, DNA molecule is an excellent example of this because it provides a blueprint for offspring to be built for physical building blocks. This is a type of replication method.

Self-preservation Instincts

This instinct is wrapped up in the DNA. These are the survival instincts we all have that help us fight to stay alive and clear of danger or violence.

Simple Psychological Reward Seeking

All creatures have a sense of pleasure and pain in their bodies which responds to the environment. Reward-seeking is a way to gravitate toward pleasure. Sometimes they can backfire and cause destructive behaviors, like drug addiction.

Exaptation

Stephen Jay Gould introduces this concept, and it refers to a trait developed for one purpose that is later used for another purpose.

Ecosystems

An ecosystem is any group of organisms coexisting in the natural world. Many ecosystems have a variety of different organisms living shoulder to shoulder. Social systems can have similar traits, and many of the same conclusions can be made about their behavior.

Niches

This is a method of competing and behaving for survival. Humans will choose a niche for which best qualified. The problem developed when others began competing for the same niche. This can cause saturation in the niche because there can only be so many people doing the same thing before the resources are exploited.

Human Nature And Judgment

Trust

Basically, society operates on trust. Trust within the family members is usually given freely, while other relationships earn trust. A system of trust works the best, and the benefits of the trust are very high.

Tendency To Feel Envy And Jealousy

Humans tend to get jealous of those who have something they don't. They believe they're owed or do the same or more. Prolonged envy or jealousy can drive a person to irrational behavior.

Denial

Denial can be powerfully destructive to the human condition. Denying reality is often a coping mechanism, but if not managed, can lead to a total detachment from reality altogether.

Tendency To Stereotype

Stereotyping is when someone generalizes and categorizes something rather than for specific traits. This is generally applied to humans.

Social Proof

Humans are a social species along with many other animals. We tend to seek safety in numbers and will look for social approval of our behavior. As a result, this gives a collaborative sense of cooperation and culture to live in a society. However, that acceptance can be withdrawn if poor behavior is deemed to be acceptable by the social whole.

Narrative Instinct

Human beings are called the storytelling animal because we have a deep-seated need to bring meaning to our lives. Before we could read or write, we were telling stories.

Curiosity Instincts

We are the most curious species of all species here. This can lead to great things, but it can also lead to our demise. We have questions about the world around us and how we got here. Curiosity leads to interesting human behavior.

Language Instinct

We use language to craft stories, as well as to gossip and solve problems. The idea that grammatical language is not a simple cultural artifact was first made famous by the linguist Noam Chomsky. It said that grammatically ordered language erratically carries infinite bearing meaning.

First Conclusion Bias

Charlie Monger observed that the mind works like a sperm and egg: the first idea I get and then the mind shuts. Speaking from a survival perspective, this is probably a device used to save energy in our bodies. We tend to settle on the first conclusion which leads to many false assumptions. That combined with the fact that we stop asking questions and many times we can be wrong about a lot of things.

Tendency To Overgeneralize From Small Samples

Human beings need to generalize. We don't have to see every scenario from beginning to end to be able to make general rules about how it works. While this can give us an initial picture, it also comes with a certain number of fallacies when we disregard the law of large numbers and act as if it doesn't exist. We will take a small number of circumstances and create a general category, even if the conclusion is not statistically backed.

Relative Satisfaction/Misery Tendencies

Relative tendencies cause either great happiness or misery in a varying array of situations and make it hard for us to predict her behavior and feelings. Human happiness studies show that happiness is related to the state of the person relative to either their past or their peers, not an absolute.

Commitment And Consistency Bias

Humans have an aversion to missing their prior commitments and not staying consistent. Humans consider this irresponsible and try to maintain the social norm. Unreliable people are often distrusted.

Hindsight bias

Once the outcome is revealed, it's almost impossible to look back in time mentally. We automatically reason that we knew the answer all along when we are actually reasoning using the set of facts we know now but not then. This is why it's essential to keep a document or journal of essential decisions to build a go back and look to evaluate it on its own merit.

Sensitivity To Fairness

Justice is a deep-seated value in our lives. We are all judges when it comes to evaluating what is fair. When someone violates that fairness, it can be considered a reason for reciprocal action, or at the very least not trust them anymore. However, fairness doesn't seem to be something that stays consistent. It depends on the collective perspective of society at any given time.

Influences Of Stress

Stress can cause physical and psychological responses and can influence other biases. Specifically, it worsens the conditions when the body goes into a fight or flight response. Stress can cause bad decisions, knee-jerk reactions, and a regression into bad habits.

Survivorship Bias

The problem with history books is that it's written by the winners. We do not see the individual lives of those who did not win. We give more credit to things done by the successful individual rather than treating it to lock; we also learn lessons steeped in fallacy by only studying the victors without seeing all of the losers who acted similarly but were not able to succeed.

Boredom Syndrome

Most humans want to act, even when they don't have to. We also want to offer solutions to problems that aren't ours, or that we don't have enough knowledge to solve the problem. This is also called the tendency to want to do something.

Falsification/Confirmation Bias

Simply put, we see what we choose to see. We look for patterns that confirm our long-held beliefs rather than unpleasant things we don't want to see. The scientific model is used to do the exact opposite which is white so effective when used correctly.

Chapter 3: Problem Solving

What you think is what you feel is the premise of cognitive psychology. Most people think that your feelings come before or are separate from your thoughts, but the truth is that your feelings are the result of your thoughts. This can either be good or bad news depending on how you feel about it.

It could be bad news because we learn that we are responsible for our moods. We can blame this on anybody else. Our attitude dictates the direction of our thoughts. It can also be liberating because we realize that we are given the power to make the choice on which perspective we want to choose to see. This, in turn, affects our mood and our thoughts as well.

When it dawns on us that we have the power to choose and focus our thinking in any direction, we realize that we have more control over the circumstances in our lives and our thoughts. This, in turn, improves our decision-making, and in general, we live much more productive lives. Isn't that great news?

That doesn't mean that we minimize the feelings that we have as humans. We don't have to suppress them in any way; this is just a way for us to balance how we feel with our scientific cognitive abilities.

Some examples of when we are thinking in a critical and problem-solving way are:

- **Rely on logic rather than emotion.** Using logic gives us an accurate picture of the problem we're trying to solve. The motion complicates everything. Stay rational and firmly set in reason.

- **Consider a wide variety of perspectives and viewpoints.** Opening up our world to other perspectives allows us to gather more of a bigger picture so that we can evaluate it and ultimately provide a more comprehensive and accurate solution.

- **Keep an open mind to interpretations that are different from our own.** We never know what little gems lie in interpreting information in several different ways.

- **Accept new findings, explanations, and evidence.** Again, this goes back to widening our perspectives and interpretations of the information we're taking in. More information allows us more options in finding the most useful solutions.

- **Willingness to reassess information to make sure it's accurate and can be seen from a variety of perspectives.** If we are set on looking at information only one way, that limits us to something we may have missed.

- **Put aside personal biases and prejudices.** This contains data when we need to have an open mind to be able to interpret information accurately.

- **Consider all realistic and reasonable possibilities.** Even those that we may not deem worthy, it's still important to consider them.

- **Avoid snap judgments.** Rushing through this process and not taking the time to find the truth can be one of the most damaging mistakes we can make in search of a solution.

Learning to think critically or solve problems takes time, perseverance, and plenty of practice. Knowing the proper steps to take and how to apply them helps master the process.

Critical thinking steps to problem-solving

As with everything else in life, problem-solving, and learning to think critically is a long-term process and takes time and a lot of practice. Understanding the steps to take and how to use them to massive the process is critical.

Identify the problem.

Before you can do anything, you need to know if a problem exists. When you sit down and consciously think about the situation, sometimes you might find that there isn't a problem at all. It may just be a miscommunication or misunderstanding. If that turns out to be the case, that's great. But if it doesn't, and you find that there is an actual legitimate problem, you must identify precisely what the problem is. The act of being able to pinpoint the problem and way out the positives and negatives of that problem is a sign of highly developed intelligence.

Look at the problem from different angles.

Once the problem has been clearly identified, it's important to analyze it for accuracy. This means that you have to look at it from several different perspectives. Is it something that can be solved? Is it a real problem or a perceived problem? Do you need help to solve this or can you solve it by yourself? When you're looking at the problem from several different angles most of the time, you can come up with a solution almost immediately. You might also uncover bias or a narrow viewpoint that needs to be expanded.

Brainstorm for possible solutions.

There are several ways the problems can be solved. Brainstorming a list of possible solutions allows our minds the freedom to produce a list of anything and everything that reveals itself. No matter how silly or strange, putting it down to paper and then reviewing the entire list to narrow it down is the best way to find the best possibilities. When you have several realistic options, you can choose the best solution.

Decide which solution works for the situation.

Review your list of possible solutions. Each situation will be different, and it will call for a different solution. In fact, many times what works in one situation would be a complete disaster and another even if they're similar situations. Taking the time to analyze which solution would work for which situation pays off and resolving the problem. One solution typically does not solve or fit every situation.

Take action.

It isn't enough to brainstorm. You have to take action if you want anything to happen. Incorporate your solution into the situation and observe what happens. Every problem has a solution even if the solution is to come to terms with the situation as it is and move forward. This is where mindset plays a part because instead of looking at problems as obstacles that can't be overcome, we can change our perspective and look at them as opportunities to improve our critical thinking and problem-solving skills.

One of the best side effects of resolving problems is that each time we do it, it increases our self-worth and confidence.

When we think critically and not only helps us handle challenges in our paths more comprehensively and intelligently, it also expands our life experiences and helps us gain a greater perspective of the bigger picture.

Chapter 4: Critical Thinking Exercises and Activities

Any leader or manager understands veritable concepts. You need to build your skills and behaviors essential for leading people. Any type of position requires you to manage, and the teams mean that you have to be able to think critically and solve problems, especially if you want to survive in a competitive marketplace.

There are four core professional skills you need to know to be a successful leader. Critical thinking skills are one part of this foursome. Of course, there are others that you can use and build off of this foundation, but here are the primary four:

1. **Critical thinking skills:** this is your ability to analyze a problem and find the solution by translating complex information into an organized and easily digestible plan.
2. **Operational skills:** this is your ability to comprehend how your company makes money and translate that understanding into profits as seamlessly as possible.
3. **Leadership skills:** this is your ability to set an example and lead others through difficult times, providing confidence where others may lack. This also requires you to be creative and resourceful when solving problems.
4. **Connecting in relating skills:** this is your ability to nurture relationships and engage successfully with various

personality types at all levels of your company.

Without this foundation, everything else would crumble. So it's essential to practice critical thinking skills to be proficient in leading people.

Critical Thinking Exercises

Have you always been stumped by riddles, puzzles, and games that require you to think outside of the box? Are you sick of being the only one unable to figure out the Sunday crossword puzzle?

Critical thinking is a skill and an art that relies on practice to improve. Critical thinking allows you to step back and see the bigger picture to be able to make better decisions about which direction you'll take. It's something that takes a lot of practice to get good at over time. The good news is that with enough practice you can master critical thinking to the point that it becomes second nature for you.

Critical thinking starts with three pillars- linking ideas, structuring arguments, and recognizing incongruences.

1. **Linking ideas:** connecting two or more ideas that are on the surface seemingly unrelated.
2. **Structuring arguments:** parts of an argument that are structured in a relevant, practical, and sound way.
3. **Recognizing incongruences:** the ability to find gaps in an argument to find the actual truth.

Six Exercises To Improve Your Critical Thinking Skills

1. **Learn from other leaders.** One of the biggest lessons you can learn is that there is no need to reinvent the wheel. Very often what we need to do is already done by several who have come

before us. All we have to do is learn from their mistakes and model what they've done to get the success they have. Reading other leaders' stories gives you the ability to be exposed to new ideas and challenge your thinking differently. Try to read at least 20 minutes every day.

2. Analyze your competitors.

Studying your competitors and trying to reverse engineer their success will give you a great amount of insight into their process. You can learn a lot by studying somebody's footprint to success. Try to understand who their target audiences are and why they focus on that group. Try to learn their philosophy and what life experiences led them to believe the way that they do. Then turn the focus on your own business and identify those same elements for your own company. Where are the gaps? Where are you doing things correctly? Ask your customers what they need and if they are happy with your service. This is an excellent exercise for you and your team to execute.

3. **In every company, there are problems that everyone ignores and that nobody fixes.** Identify one of those problems, take it under your wing, and ask for support when trying to solve it. If part of the problem is beyond your scope, put together a team to help you. Guide your team through the process of analyzing information, interviewing relevant participants, and developing a potential plan of action. In addition to establishing credibility as a problem solver, you will be actively exercising all four of your professional skill sets with this exercise.

4. **Find out what keeps your customer awake at night.** You want to solve a problem that your customers are having, but not just any problem. You want to solve the problem that's so painful to them that they want it solved yesterday. How do you do that? You pick your boss's brain and find out what strategies

he uses to do this. Then you model his success and incorporate it into your process. Ask for his support as you try to meet the needs of your customers. This process will give you valuable insight into how to fulfill the needs of the people you serve. You'll not only tend to make more money, but you will realize you have a greater purpose.

5. Assign a team to it. Guide your team through the problem-solving activity. Work with them to assess the problems in your company and encourage them to have multiple perspectives about it. Share these perspectives and develop a laundry list of solutions. Frame this as an opportunity for your team to gain a wealth of insights as a result of solving the problem. Remember the saying two heads are better than one? This absolutely applies in this case. Also, be sure to reframe any challenges into opportunities so that your brain can begin thinking in a different way from the perspective of positive rather than negative.

6. Track your progress. You should log everything in. Your challenges, triumphs, and failures. This documents the experience and allows you to refer back to it for future projects. It also can help you save a lot of time from going in circles. Combine knowledge with the tactics you've already tried and which ones you've left out. You gain a tremendous amount of insight into your own critical thinking process, specifically your strengths and weaknesses.

Practical Exercises

As an adult, you know how easy it is to make a false assumption and restate it as truth. Many times we don't challenge what is being said before passing it along. We need to question authority more often, verifying that our assumptions are based on truth and not a fallacy. Here are a few exercises to enhance critical thinking skills and test those assumptions and fallacies.

Linking Ideas exercise

Grab an old-fashioned newspaper. Scroll through all the articles in each section of the newspaper. Get out a piece of paper and pencil and write down a list of the articles in the newspaper. Now look for commonalities between the articles and try to see if you can establish a connection among them. Trying to see if you can identify an overall theme for each section of a paper. If successful, see if you can connect the sections of the newspaper.

Lastly, summarize the aim of this publication and its primary innovation.

Structuring Argument

Before we get into the exercise two concepts need to be familiar with:

Premise: a proposition from which another is implied or follows as a conclusion. If the foundation of an argument, undertaking, or theory.

Conclusion: the final takeaway from an argument. A decision is reached by the process of reasoning.

Go to Google or YouTube and look for speeches on arguments and theories. Pick a couple and determine the premise of the subject as well as the conclusion. There may be more than one premise, but they have to support the conclusion.

Recognizing Incongruences

Use the same information from the previous exercise and see if you can determine whether any of the premises do not support or link to the conclusion. If all the premises are connected with the conclusion, take a more in-depth look at the premises themselves. There may be fallacies in the premises. If that's the case, do more research to see if he can get to the bottom of the actual. Lastly, analyze the premise to verify that

a false statement has not been
assumed true.

Tell It To An Alien

This can be applied to any theory or
information, but as an exercise, you're
going to look for the 10 most interesting
theories on the Internet. You'll be
playing two parts: yourself and an alien
from outer space who's never been to
Earth. You're going to try to explain this
topic to both people.

Try to explain it to the alien who has no
prior knowledge of Earth, although the
alien will speak English. Then adopt an
alien persona and ask questions about

the topic from the perspective of having no prior knowledge about it. For example, you would explain the game of bowling as one round sphere with three holes in it rolled on the ground to hit as many strange pillars as possible. When you're playing the part of the alien, you would ask questions to gain clarity and understanding.

https://blog.mindvalley.com/critical-thinking-exercises/

Activities: Question Standards To Ask

Before you know what critical thinking questions you need to ask, you're going to need to know how to ask these questions because they are critical to critical thinking.

Open-Ended Questioning

Your goal when asking questions is to prevent the person you're questioning from giving you a few details. You want them to give you as much information as possible. Yes or no answers can drag out the questioning process and unnecessarily delay getting the information you wish to have.

Therefore asking the right questions will not only give you the answers you're looking for but also lead to more questions than what you were initially looking for. Ask open-ended questions similar to the ones below:

- "What is the purpose of this product?" Instead of "Is this the purpose of this product?"
- "Who is your favorite person in all the world?" Instead of "Is this your favorite person in the whole world?"

Avoid Leading Questions

Leading questions can inject bias into the information-collecting process. Critical thinking is about getting out of your head and seeing things from a different perspective. Ideally, from the perspective of the world. It's essential to avoid leading questions so as not to taint the answer with your preconceived notions. Make sure your questions are as neutral as possible and don't allow any kind of definitive language into the questioning process. Look at the examples below:

- "What is your opinion on the healthiest exercise plan on the market?" Instead of "Don't you think the Power 90 is the healthiest exercise plan on the market?"
- "Is the condition of your family's home at the moment?" Instead of "How bad is the condition of your family's home at the moment?"

Be Specific With The Boundaries Of Your Questions

A leading question can damage your goal to find the information you want. So can leaving the question too open. It can invite unnecessary information to be given. When you're a critical thinker, that means you're objective when taking in different forms of information. However, critical thinking still needs a focus and direction that only you can control. Make sure that the skeleton outline is accurate before you shape your questions and have them answered. Being too general makes the process of getting the answers you want slow. Maybe you will have better success if you ask questions like:

- "Who is your favorite celebrity movie star in the United States?" Instead of "Who is your favorite celebrity?"
- "If you could live anywhere in Los Angeles, where would that be?" Instead of "If you could live

anywhere in the United States,
where would that be?"

Lead the questions down the funnel until you get the answer you're searching for

Shallow questions make it easy for the people you're questioning to avoid giving you the information you want. It's important to dig deeper after each question stays on the trail of the information you really want. When you get your answer, then move back to broader questioning to get an overview of the whole situation again.

All Answers Must Be Based On Facts And Supported From Many Different Sources

Hearsay is a dangerous concept. You have to make sure that you're not quoting what you heard someone else say. Find actual case studies, facts, and proof before you settle on the information you have been given. Make sure you're cross-checking the information you find to verify it's credible Put yourself in the position of the opposition and see if you can validate what they're saying as well.

Critical Thinking Method Questions

The H and the 4W's

The who, what, where, when, why, and how are the basics of critical thinking questions. It is a statistical certainty that you've learned them in school. They are the base upon which every critical analysis should be generated. Here's how you should apply these questions to critical thinking:

- Who is responsible?
- Who with this hurt?
- Who would benefit?
- Who has looked into this before me?

- What would be the challenges?
- What are its strengths?
- What is the other perspective?
- What is the key subject?

- Where are there similar situations?
- Where can this be improved upon?
- Where can more information be found?
- Wherewith this problem reside?

- When could this be implemented?
- When is it time to stop this action?
- When is this acceptable and unacceptable?
- When would we be able to measure the result?

- Why is this relevant?
- Why is there a need for this?
- Why is this a problem?
- Why should this be made known?

- How does it function?
- How could it harm anyone?
- How is this different from anything else similar to it?
- How does it function?

Method And Agenda Questioning

Even though these two may have been covered through the 5W's and the H's, it's still worth breaking them down to emphasize the angle at which this questioning comes from.

The agenda is positioned to figure out how an individual could reap the benefit from an idea or situation. For example, if a celebrity was trying to repair their reputation and held a free charity event, then the donations would be less of a charitable intention and more about the celebrity's reputation.

To clarify an agenda, some questions that might be helpful could look like this:

- What is the individual involved trying to accomplish?
- What problems are raised by the individual involved?
- What evidence, experiences, and/or data is provided?
- How can we see from their perspective to appreciate their viewpoint?

The second part of this is questioning the method. Being a critical thinker means that the method makes the outcomes of every situation and idea questionable. Too often, the validity gets overlooked in focus on the debate when talking about the outcome of a specific method. Questions that might help clarify the method would be:

- Is the individual willing to rethink their methods of creating the outcome?

- As the individual thought about how the method will function in the future?
- How far has the method been tested?
- Is there an alternative method that can be used to produce the same outcome and what would the implications of using this method?
- Is the individual willing to allow this method to be tested?
- Are there other situations this method has been used and if so, how effective was it?

The Inquiry Process

It does what the title states. It contains some questions, but the effectiveness of this process lies in the way this process is conducted. This process creates an order that you can follow while uncovering the information you're looking for. The terminology may vary,

but the foundation remains the same.
The process is broken up into five parts:

- Ask (pose a question)
- Investigate (find resources)
- Create (interpret/synthesize)
- Discuss (report findings)
- Reflect (reverse engineer the process)

https://blog.mindvalley.com/critical-thinking-questions/

Chapter 5: Critical Thinking in Everyday Life Situations

The journey to becoming a better critical thinker is joined by the process of accelerating personal growth. When you are as your point gets better, you can begin to see where you can improve and grow.

The following examples can be applied to your everyday routine. They will allow you to really start critically thinking and discover the art of questioning everything around you. Look at the examples below of how critical thinking affects your everyday life:

Self Reflection-taking Inventory Of Your Shortcomings

By researching and issuing cultural differences, you begin to empathize with people from other cultures and start seeing where they're coming from.

Self-reflection on your behavior in a particular incident with another individual, you begin to see things from their perspective and realize there were a few things you could have done differently to yield a more favorable result.

Upon completion of a task, you think back to what you've learned and how you could have made better decisions to get more experience from the situation.

Decision-making- More Educated Decision-making

Thinking back to an altercation with someone you care about you start seeing things from their perspective. This dissolves your feelings, and you can see a panoramic picture of the situation as a whole. From this spot, you can make a more purposeful decision in the future.

You are asked to create a mockup of the future residential neighborhood next to an industrial area sitting next to a river. Your research leads you to play out scenarios in your head on the pros and cons of the projects and from the perspective of the people in the neighborhood, and the environmental effects this project will have on the earth. Once you see all sides, you can make a more educated and logical decision.

Time Utilization Analysis - recognize Your Value

You take stock of what you do in a day and how long it takes you to do it. You notice that there's a lot of time being wasted watching movies. You decide to narrow down your movie time by watching only one good movie per day and use the extra time to tackle another goal like practicing your writing.

You look at your to-do list and break down the priority of each task. You evaluate each task to see how it affects the largest group of people. With this information, you begin to focus and spend more time on the most important tasks first.

Workplace Critical Thinking Examples

Teamwork-problem-solving As A Group

You have been promoted to project leader in your department. It's your responsibility to come up with a strategy to produce a new product. You give the entire team the authority to write down all concerns they may have, as well as solution recommendations, and constructively criticize other solutions. Simultaneously, you have someone jotting down notes. At one point, he stopped the conversation and wrote all the notes on the board divided into perspectives and obstacles. You and your team can now clearly create a solution based on the collaborative information given by your team.

Adding Value Improving And Recognizing Your Contribution

Your company has its eye on achieving a certain goal by the end of the year. You take stock of your position at the company and think about ways that you can contribute toward this goal. Make a list of every way that your actions can help achieve this goal and then credit the impact of each action to the person or area that is impacting. Then you think about all the ways that you could add more action to increase the productivity and impact on the goal.

https://blog.mindvalley.com/critical-thinking-examples/
https://www.wabisabilearning.com/blog/critical-thinking-exercises-blow-students-minds

Chapter 6: Goal Setting

What exactly is a goal?

A goal is something you hope to achieve that will elevate your present situation. When you set out to make a goal for yourself, you take into account who you are, the environment around you, the skills you have, and the things you desire. In essence, setting a goal represents critical thinking and action.

As you work toward your goal, you're continually analyzing your progress as well as acknowledging the challenges in your way so that you can create strategies to overcome them.

Goals are kind of like a roadmap toward success. Some are long-term others short-term. Sometimes you have to set several goals to meet your ultimate goal.

For example, if you want to be a doctor, you have to set another long-term goal of finishing college and medical school. To graduate, you need to achieve short-term goals like passing the required courses necessary to graduate. The short and long-term goals are linked together like a chain, each reliant on the other to achieve your ultimate success.

Understanding how to use critical thinking to create and achieve your goals is fundamental. There is a five-step process for setting up any goal, and every step demands that you implement critical thinking skills. Let's get into detail to see how this overall process runs.

Step One: Gather Information About Yourself

The very first thing you need to know is information about yourself in terms of what you'd like to accomplish and your strengths so that you're able to have goals that are easily defined, realistic, manageable, and meaningful to you. The first thing you want to do is take inventory of your strengths and weaknesses. Review the challenges you encounter daily in your life, both personal and professional. Then recall any past experiences you've had. Determine whether you want your goal to focus on the strengths or weaknesses that you have. For example, if you're unhappy that you procrastinate, then a solution would be to set a goal of small baby steps of improvement to get your work done without overwhelming yourself.

Step Two: Set A SMART Goal

Once you've gathered information about yourself, the next thing you want to do is set a goal that displays what you want to achieve. It should be a SMART goal-- specific, measurable, achievable, relevant to you personally, and time-limited.

You should not have a vague goal by any means. Saying, "I'm going to get more rest," is weak and does nothing to motivate you to achieve it. It also makes it difficult to know whether or not you have achieved it.
Goals that are vacant without definable limits and boundaries and leave you in the sense of limbo never knowing when you've crossed the finish line.

That's why the SMART approach allows you to create goals that are strong and definable and realistically able to be achieved through detailed steps.

Specific. Having a specific cold-like "get eight hours of sleep per night" contrast against a vague goal "get more sleep," gives you defined boundaries and a clear understanding of what the goal is and when you've achieved it.

Measurable. The best way to tell the goal is measurable is that you know when you've reached it. It's a specific point on your journey. For example, when you reach a certain number on the scale, you can tell that you've lost weight.

Achievable. When making goals you want to make sure that your goal is achievable and not out of your reach. That's the most frustrating thing that happens to us when we don't realize what we've been striving for is realistically possible at that particular time. This is different for each individual. For example, wanting to lose 100 pounds in the next week may not be an achievable or realistic goal. On the other hand, completing a course may be achievable. If there's any question in your mind about whether your goals are achievable, perhaps you'd want to retake a look at your goal and evaluate it to make sure that it is reasonable to achieve in the time that you set for it. Then once you accomplish that goal, you can set the standard higher for yourself. Find the balance between your goals being challenging enough to motivate and inspire you but not so challenging that it's impossible to reach them.

Relevant to you. Goals should reflect your personal values, career plans, and interests. They have to be personalized specifically to you and no one else. This makes them extremely motivated to want to pursue. It's how you know you're doing it for yourself versus for anybody else. So if you love math and you want to become a rocket scientist, the motivation will be easier for you to reach that goal of studying those hard classes.

Time-limited. SMART goals must have deadlines or else they're just wishes. A goal has to have a definite time limit to set the action in motion. However, make sure the deadline isn't too far away that you will procrastinate or lose interest in it. On the flip side, if you set a deadline that's too early, the goal may start to seem like pressure and unachievable. This can lead to major overwhelm and discouragement. Setting a fair and realistic time limit for achieving your goal is going to help you figure out if you've achieved it.

Step Three: Make A Plan Of Action

You need a plan of action if you're going to accomplish anything. Goals are no different. These are a list of steps or can take to achieve your goal and the order in which you'll take them. It's kind of like a to-do list for reaching your goal.

Write your actions down.
When developing a plan of action, The first step is to write down the actions; you'll be taking to reach your goal. You might say that you have a list in your head, but writing it down on paper is going to serve you better. That's because we often forget, despite the fact we tell ourselves we aren't going to, we do forget. According to a recent study, 43% of participants who didn't write their goals down actually achieved their goals. Compared to 76% of participants who wrote their goals down and achieved them, that's quite a

difference. It doesn't matter if the list is incomplete sentences or perfect. You just want to get the thoughts down on paper.

Prioritize your steps. Once you brainstorm every possible step that you can take, and write it down, decide which steps are more important and which ones are of lesser importance. You determine this by evaluating whether this step is critical to the goal. If you can't achieve your goal without taking that step, it's critical. If you can achieve your goal without taking that step, it is not critical. The items that are not critical should be the lowest on the list.

List your steps in order and set deadlines once you organize the critical and noncritical steps on your list or range steps in the order in which you'll complete them. Make sure you have a deadline for each step so that you can stay on track to your ultimate goal.

Step Four: List Barriers And Solutions

Barriers are going to pop up regardless of how prepared you are or how rock solid your plan of action is for accomplishing your goal. A barrier is something that keeps you from making progress toward your goal. It could be anything like your own tendency to procrastinate, for example, or something out of your control, like an unforeseen tragedy — their barriers that you can control and others you can't. As you establish your goals, get in front of the barriers by writing down possible barriers you could encounter. When you see the potential barriers, you can plan for them, or at least not be caught off guard if they pop up. You can also plan in advance for how you will deal with them if they happen. For example, if you take on too many clients, you might be able to predict that you will have enough time to fill all the orders you promised. By anticipating this barrier, you can figure out ways to avoid getting into that situation-such as outsourcing part of the job and paying somebody else to do it. There's nothing that says you have to confront these barriers by yourself. There are several resources around you that you can take advantage of. All you have to do is look around.

Step Five: Act And Evaluate Outcomes

As you drive down the journey of your plan of action steps toward your goal, evaluate your progress regularly. Are the steps you're on getting you closer to your goal or further away? Are they effective? Are you going to complete them on time? Is the plan as a whole helping you get closer to meeting your goal? If you find yourself falling behind, the process of evaluating your outcomes helps you tweak your plan of action sooner rather than later so that you can change to accommodate these factors. It keeps you on track. Evaluation can also keep you motivated to continue working toward your goal. Make sure that you're celebrating small wins along the way. This goes a long way to motivate you as well. Sometimes she will have setbacks. You must know this now so that you can anticipate when it happens. Also, you want to stay positive. The point of evaluating your progress is to deal with and identify setbacks. The more practice you have doing this, the better you'll get at not letting the setbacks derail your progress.

Chapter 7: Conclusion

By now, you should have everything you need to begin your journey to better critical thinking skills. Remember that in addition to the principles we covered in this book, the central element that takes you from an unreflective thinker to a master thinker is practice. This is something you can't do sporadically. You have to make it part of your daily routine.

In Chapter 1, we discovered the six stages of critical thinkers: unreflective thinkers, challenged thinkers, beginning thinkers, practicing thinkers, advanced thinkers, and master thinkers. We broke those down into six different categories: defining a feature, principal challenge, knowledge of thinking, skill in thinking, relevant intellectual traits, and some implications for instruction. We determined the definition of critical thinking and how it can benefit you in your daily life. In order to do that, we were able to establish the four assumptions of critical thinking.

In Chapter 2, we discussed the concept of mental toughness and the elemental structures in thinking which are clarity, accuracy, precision, relevance, depth, breadth, logic, significance, and fairness. We also discussed the various mental models that can be used when developing critical thinking skills.

In Chapter 3, we identified steps to problem-solving which include: identifying the problem, looking at the problem from different angles, brainstorming for possible solutions, deciding which solution works for the situation, and taking action. These straightforward steps are the key to solving almost any problem.

In Chapter 4, we put our knowledge of critical thinking to the test by reviewing specific exercises and activities to get us practicing daily. We learned that there are four core professional skills: critical thinking, operational thinking, leadership thinking, connecting, and relating thinking. There are also three pillars to critical thinking: linking ideas, structuring arguments, and recognizing incongruences.

We learned that there were six exercises to improve critical thinking skills: learning from other leaders, analyzing our competitors, and every company there are problems that everyone ignores and nobody fixes, finding out what keeps your customer awake at night, assigning a team to it, and tracking your progress.

Chapter 5 was all about critical thinking in everyday life situations. We took a look at real-world examples of how critical thinking could benefit our lives and work and at home. This included:

taking inventory of our shortcomings, more educated decision-making, recognizing our value, problem-solving as a group, and recognizing our contribution.

Chapter 6 was entirely about goal setting. We determined the definition of what a goal is and how to obtain it. We established that there are five steps to goal setting: gathering information about yourself, setting a SMART goal, (making sure that goal is specific, measurable, achievable, relevant to you, and time-limited.), Making a plan of action, listing barriers and solutions and acting and evaluating outcomes.

With time and a lot of practice, you could build your critical thinking skills to a master thinker. This means you would be able to see a variety of perspectives other than your own critically and analyze them to make the best decisions in all areas of your life.

The bottom line, if you want to succeed in today's busy world, you have to become a critical thinker. Great business leaders and managers know this, and they work every day to perfect their thinking process.

The person who can solve the problems is the person who is going to pay the most. Being able to decipher solutions in the middle of a difficult problem is the person everyone will go to. You can leverage your critical thinking skills into a great life, a good life, and valuable relationships.

Make sure that you question assumptions. Critical thinkers are inquisitive they look to find why something is happening and what's behind every problem — critical thinkers of the ones who get us out of economic hardship and invent ways to prosper.

Adopts different perspectives. Take the road less traveled. You won't get noticed if you're following the crowd. Think outside of the box and dare to do what nobody else is doing. Analyze the world around you see what others are doing that works for them and copy it.

See the potential in yourself. Realize that these simple skills and not something you're born with. You can do this. You can get better at it and master it, but you have to practice. Critical thinkers have confidence that allows them to see opportunities where others see challenges. They don't give up without a fight.

Managing ambiguity. The speed of business is intertwined with global factors and complicated dichotomies where knowing all the variables is impossible. One significant trait of a critical thinker is that they are comfortable with operating in an environment where change is constant fast-thinking decisions need to be made. If you can win yourself to that kind of pressure, not only are you serving the greater good but you will most certainly be compensated for it.

Critical thinking has always been highly regarded as a trait of leadership, but over the years schools have dropped the importance of critical thinking in favor of quantitative skills. However, the need for critical thinking is in high demand now more than ever.

The world is growing crowded, and we don't know when the next economic downturn can happen. But one thing is sure; we need critical thinkers who can see the situation for what it is and provide solutions where others may not and cannot see it.

Visit: https://criticalthinkingsecrets.com/

www.ingramcontent.com/pod-product-compliance
Lightning Source LLC
Chambersburg PA
CBHW051347280526
45784CB00007B/2845